# The PRISM Workbook

## A PRrogram for Innovative Self-Management

*David B. Wexler, Ph.D.*

W. W. NORTON • *NEW YORK* • *LONDON*

This book contains exercises to be used in the 16-group program described in **The Adolescent Self**



**Library of Congress Cataloging-in-Publication Data**

Wexler, David B.
The prism workbook : a program for innovative self-management / David B. Wexler.
p. cm.
ISBN 0-393-70119-0
1. Self-actualization (Psychology) 2. Self-management (Psychology) 3. Self-management (Psychology)—Problems, exercises, etc. 4. Control (Psychology) I. Title.
BF637.S4W45 1991 158'.1—dc20 91-9530

W. W. Norton & Company, Inc., 500 Fifth Avenue, New York, N.Y. 10110
W. W. Norton & Company, Inc., 10 Coptic Street, London WC1A 1PU

7 8 9

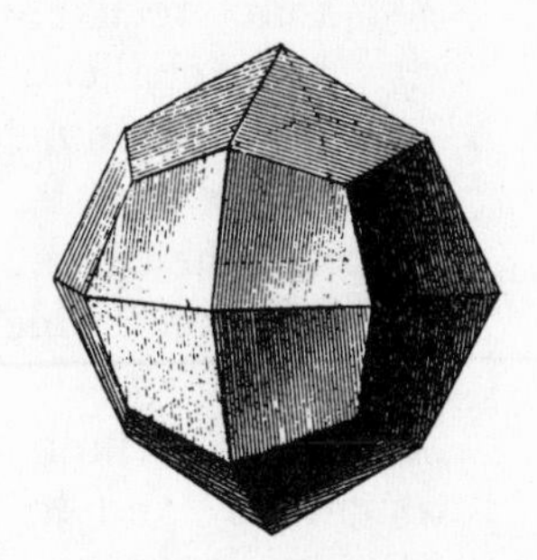

# Welcome to PRISM

The purpose of this PRogram for Innovative Self-Management is to help you develop new skills in self-management. For those of you who do things under stress that you later regret (like using drugs or alcohol, getting into fights, hurting yourself, running away, stealing things, breaking things, saying things you don't mean, etc.), this program can help you develop better control over your behavior. For those of you who easily get depressed, angry, or anxious, self-management means developing better control over your thoughts and feelings.

Throughout these group sessions, you will learn the basic building blocks for self-management:

1. Self-Talk: You will gain more control over how you talk to yourself so you can have more control over your own feelings and reactions.
2. Self-Soothing: You will develop skills in how to calm your body down when you feel stressed or explosive. You will learn how to "slow time down."
3. Self-Expression (Assertiveness): You will learn how to let other people know what you are feeling and what you need in ways

that are likely to work. You will learn to handle more and more challenging situations so that you end up feeling powerful rather than helpless.

Power is the main point here. We would like you to gain a sense of "empowerment," which is the ability to take charge and to not be a victim.

All of the techniques are designed to help you stop doing things automatically and to increase your abilities for personal choice. In PRISM, no one is trying to tell you what you should do. We are simply making sure that you are aware of all your options.

# Contents

GROUP 1

# Introduction to Self-Talk/ABCDE

In this first group, it is important to understand the basic ABCDE model of thoughts and feelings.

First Event

Imagine any event, like when you sit down to lunch in the cafeteria, and someone else gets up to leave at the same time.

Self-Talk

Now, imagine what you might say to yourself. Some of you might say, "That guy must not like me. What did I do wrong?"

Feelings and Behaviors

Now think about how you would feel and act if you said this to yourself. You would probably feel depressed and rejected; you might act angry or withdrawn.

New Self-Talk

However, you might not have interpreted this correctly. Each of us has a pattern of automatic "self-talk"—this often keeps us stuck with bad feelings. Another kind of self-talk might have been, "I wonder why he's leaving. He seems to like me, so I don't think it's because of me. Maybe he had to go do something."

New Feelings and Behaviors

How would you feel and act if you thought like this instead? You probably wouldn't have many feelings one way or the other, but you certainly wouldn't feel depressed or rejected. You wouldn't have any reason to act withdrawn or angry. You might even act concerned and try to find out if he was upset about something.

The point of this is that *the way we talk to ourselves controls how we feel and act*. We are all talking to ourselves all the time—the goal here is to gain more control over this self-talk.

Here is another example:

First Event

Your parents are fighting over money.

Self-Talk

You say to yourself, "If they didn't have to support me, they would be happier. This is my fault." This (as you will soon discover) is known as an "Error in Blaming."

Feelings and Behaviors

With this self-talk, you would probably feel depressed and guilty. You might even feel angry that you are a burden to them (or so you think). You might withdraw or think of running away, or you might do something to try and take away the bad feelings, like getting high.

### D New Self-Talk

A different kind of self-talk might be, "I wish they would get along better, but I know it's not my fault."

### E New Feelings and Behaviors

With this self-talk, you would feel concerned but not responsible. You might want to just stay away while they are fighting about this and realize that you're not directly involved with this problem.

In the following pages, you will find a list of seven categories of faulty self-talk. All of these are typical ways that we distort events. The payoffs for challenging some of this faulty self-talk are reduced stress, reduced depression, reduced anxiety, more confidence, more trust of others, and improved relationships.

## FAULTY SELF-TALK

1. BLACK AND WHITE: The tendency to see things in an all or nothing fashion. Beware of words like "never," "always," "nothing," and "everyone."

   "Cool kids use; if you don't use, you're a nerd!"
   "You're either on my side or not."
   "You can't trust anyone over 30!"

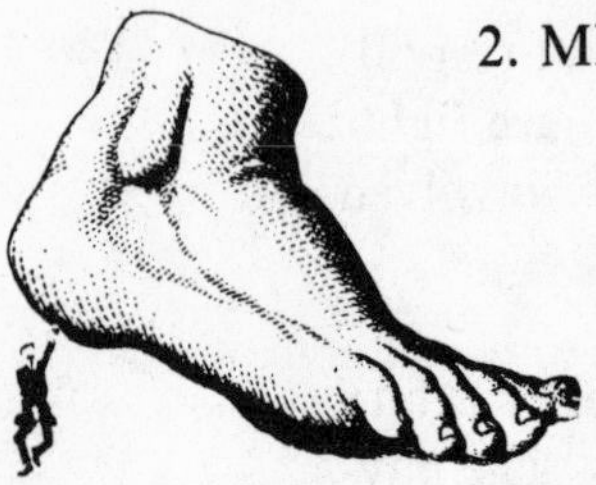

2. MINIMIZING: The tendency to downplay your achievements.

   "Even though I finally made Level 3, it's no big thing."
   "I did well, but so did a lot of other people."
   "The staff just gives me good feedback because they're paid to say it."
   "That guy likes me, but the really rad one doesn't."

3. MINDREADING: The tendency to assume that others think something of you without checking it out.

   "I know she hates me . . . she gave me a dirty look."
   "She's avoiding me . . . she must be pretty mad at me."
   "My mom didn't call me . . . she must not care about me."
   "Those guys didn't eat lunch with me . . . they must think I'm a real geek."

4. AWFULIZING: The tendency to predict that things will turn out "awful" for you.

   "When I go home, I know I'm going to mess up big time."
   "I'll never make it to Level 3."
   "Staff will never trust me again."
   "I know I'm not going to make it through this place."

5. ERRORS IN BLAMING: The tendency to unfairly blame yourself or others.

   "It's all my fault." or "It's all their fault."
   "It's my fault my father drinks."
   "I was molested because of something I did wrong."
   "You always mess everything up for me."

6. DOWN-PUTTING: The tendency to put yourself down for having one problem or making one mistake.

   "I'm overweight, so I must be lazy and stupid."
   "I failed this test, I must be dumb."
   "I'm in counseling, I must be a bad kid."
   "She doesn't like me, I must be ugly."

7. EMOTIONAL REASONING: The tendency to conclude that if you feel a certain way about yourself, then it must be true.

   "Since I feel bad about myself, I must be a bad person."
   "I feel rejected, so everybody must be rejecting me."
   "Since I feel guilty, I must have done something wrong."

## FAULTY SELF-TALK QUIZ I

Each of the following statements falls into a category of faulty self-talk. Which one?

1. The counselor told me I'm doing better, but I know he tells that to everybody.
2. I *feel* lonely, so I guess nobody likes me.
3. Ever since Linda hurt me, I know that all redheads can't be trusted.
4. Nothing's ever going to work out for me.
5. It's your fault we never do anything fun.
6. My parents got divorced—it must have been something about me.
7. I sometimes don't get things right so I must be lazy or stupid.

## STAIRWAY

Imagine yourself standing on the top of a 10-step stairway, any kind you want. With each breath, count backwards from 10 to 1 as you visualize yourself walking down the stairs, becoming more relaxed with each step.

> Optional: You can continue this exercise by imagining that you have arrived at a special, personal place; then explore this place in your mind.

GROUP 2

# New Self-Talk

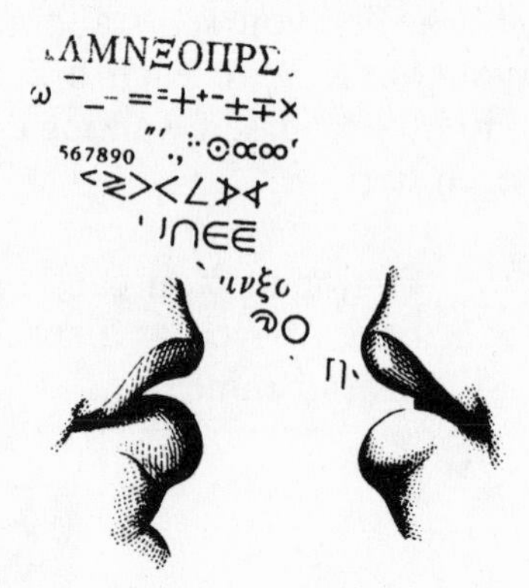

In this group, we will continue to help you understand how self-talk can control your feelings and behaviors.

After enough practice with these, you will see how your beliefs control your feelings—and how much difference it can make when you think differently. Remember: The goal is *self-management*. The more you know about what your mind is doing, the more personal power you have.

When trying to think of new new self-talk, keep in mind these principles:

- Is the new thought *specific*? Instead of "always" and "totally," think in terms of "in this situation" and "sometimes."
- Is the new thought *accurate*? It has to be true or else it won't work.
- Is the new thought *too good to be true*? You can't replace "I'm such a jerk" with "I'm the greatest guy in the world!" Your inner mind will never believe you. You have to stay realistic.
- Is the new thought *assuming* something? You can't read other people's minds—and when you try, you may often think the worst.
- Is it *positive*?
- Is it *productive*?

## FAULTY SELF-TALK QUIZ II

Which category of faulty self-talk is illustrated by each of the following statements?

1. He's always smiling, but I know he doesn't like me.
2. I hurt my mother's feelings, so I must be an evil person.
3. I work so hard, and I can tell from the way people look at me that nobody appreciates me.
4. If you weren't so uptight about everything, our relationship would be great.
5. Anybody who needs something from other people is weak.
6. I just know this "pass" is going to turn out terrible.
7. Although I did well in school, I'm not really smart.
8. I saw my father get angry and out of control, so anytime someone gets angry things will get out of control.

## FAULTY SELF-TALK SITUATIONS

In the next exercise, circle the faulty self-talk in each example.

1. You're supposed to have a big softball game today. It's raining, so the game is cancelled. You say "We're never going to play. Nothing is ever going to work out around here!"

   a. Awfulizing b. Minimizing c. Down-putting
   d. Emotional reasoning e. Mind-reading

2. Her boyfriend looked up from across the table and said, "Oh, yeah, that's interesting." She said to herself, "I know he is dying for lunch to be over so he can get away from me."

   a. Error in blaming b. Minimizing c. Awfulizing
   d. Black and White e. Mind-reading

3. A teenage boy was angry about his 11:00 p.m. curfew. He was worried that other kids wouldn't think he was "cool." When a girl he liked didn't want to go out with him, he yelled at his parents, "It's your fault she doesn't like me!"

   a. Minimizing b. Black and White c. Error in blaming
   d. Down-putting e. Awfulizing

## FALLING LEAF

Stare at a point on the wall across from you. Visualize a leaf at that spot. With each breath, count backwards from 20 to 1 as you watch the leaf very slowly drifting to the ground. At 1, the leaf reaches the ground and you are very deeply relaxed.

GROUP 3

# Introduction to Observers

In this group, we introduce a new concept: the Observer.*

At first, it may be difficult to realize how much we talk to ourselves all the time. Inside of each of us are many "observers" who decide how we're going to react to a particular situation. In this week's group, we will learn about three typical "observers" who can easily take over. The three "observers" are the Resentful Observer, the Hopeless Observer, and the Self-Critical Observer. As you will see, these very familiar "observers" can make us feel depressed, unmotivated, anxious, or frustrated.

However, we also each carry another kind of Observer inside: the Supportive Observer. This observer is your ally, which many of you may have learned about in your individual PRISM sessions.

An ally is someone who is on your side and someone you can count on when you need him or her. This Supportive Observer is available to talk back to the "negative observers." For most of us, the Supportive Observer that we carry with us is modeled after someone we have known. It may be a blend of several people who have served as allies.

You may notice similarities between some of the things these "observers" say and some of the faulty self-talk we've discussed in the previous weeks. See how many of these you can identify.

*Adapted from Wilson, R. R. (1986). *Don't panic*. New York: Harper & Row.

## THE RESENTFUL OBSERVER

- blames others;
- is convinced that he or she is being treated unfairly;
- has a short fuse and gets irritated easily;
- usually feels tense and bitter.

**Frustration/Anger**

- "I can't ever get a fair deal around here."
- "Nobody ever listens to me."
- "Why won't you do it *my* way?"

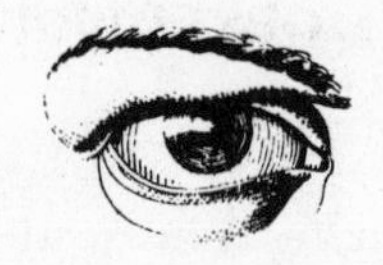

## THE SELF-CRITICAL OBSERVER

- makes certain you understand what a failure you are;
- reminds you of past mistakes;
- points out all of your flaws regularly, in case you might have forgotten;
- uses any mistake to remind you of how bad you are.

**Low Self-Esteem/Low Motivation**

- "I'm doing terribly. I'm a weak person and a total failure."
- "It's typical that I screwed up! When am I going to grow up and face the world?"
- "I messed things up in my family again. All I do is cause trouble! I've always been like this."

## THE HOPELESS OBSERVER

- believes there is something totally wrong with you;
- expects you to fail in the future just as you have failed in the past;
- expects that you will continue to be deprived and frustrated;
- believes that life will never be fair to you.

**Depression**

- "I wanted to get some work done . . . why bother? I won't do well anyway."
- "I was going to tell my counselor I was upset, but I'll just get in trouble. Nothing ever works out for me."
- "I can't ever please my parents so I might as well not try to do anything right."

## THE SUPPORTIVE OBSERVER (THE ALLY)

Instead of filtering events through these negative observers, an alternative is to turn to your Supportive Observer. The Supportive Observer

- reminds you of your freedom and choices;
- supports all your efforts;
- expects a positive future, reminds you of the positives in your past;
- trusts you and lets you trust yourself;
- focuses more on solution then on problems.

**Safety, Confidence, Support**

- "Even though I didn't make it, I tried my best."
- "I know I've had successes before and I can have them again."
- "I'm beginning to feel uptight, but I've learned ways to handle this."
- "Maybe I couldn't handle talking to my parents before, but I've learned more options and skills now."
- "How can I help solve this problem rather than blame myself or someone else?"

## TEN CANDLES

Close your eyes and imagine a row of ten lit candles in front of you, any style or color. As you exhale, imagine yourself blowing out one of the candles. With each successive breath, blow out each candle and let yourself become more deeply relaxed with each one. When all the candles are out, let yourself enjoy the peace and quiet of the room.

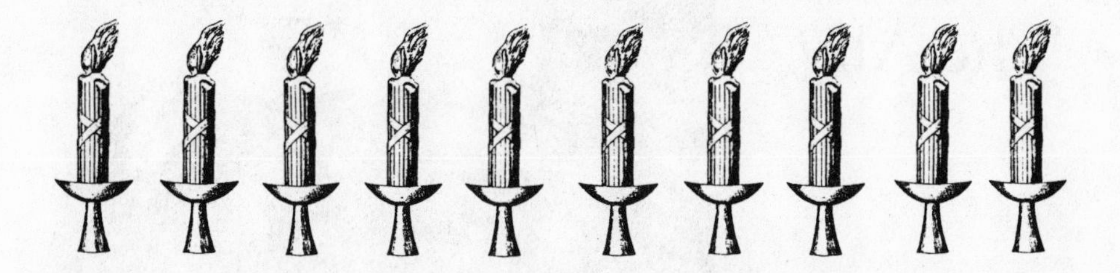

GROUP 4

# The Ally

Now that you have had some exposure to the Supportive Observer that we introduced last week, it is time to learn some more about your ally.

As you remember, your ally is someone who is on your side and someone you can always count on. The ally can be a coach, a guide, a teacher, or a special friend. If a person has a soothing or supportive effect on you, he or she is probably an ally. An ally is someone you carry around inside of you who knows just what to say or do: how to comfort you when you're sad, praise you when you do something well, and hang in there with you when you are angry.

Today's group will focus on giving you more practice with the Supportive Observer—otherwise known as the ally. You will get a chance to practice being an ally to each other, then visualize ways that you can be a better ally to yourself.

## THE THREE ALLIES

Before you begin, think for a moment about people who have helped you as an ally in the past. Now sit quietly and take several deep, relaxing breaths.

Now recall a childhood experience when you felt particularly sad. Imagine the ally figure that we have been talking about. Picture exactly how your ally could have been the most help to you at that moment. Now focus inward and just notice the effects of the ally in your scene.

Repeat the same visualization, except this time recall a time when you felt particularly proud or excited. Imagine your ally responding to you.

Finally, repeat this scene with a memory of a situation when you felt very angry and frustrated. Imagine your ally helping you through this.

GROUP 5

# Introduction to Assertiveness

Now we move into another important area of coping skills and stress management:communication. This next series of groups is designed to teach you assertiveness.

It is very easy to feel depressed or angry when you feel powerless. If you don't have effective ways of making yourself heard and of getting your needs met, the world seems threatening and frustrating. Learning assertiveness increases your odds of making the world more satisfying and having more self-respect.

The two basic rules in assertiveness training are the following:

1. Express your own feelings and needs
2. in a way that is direct, nonjudgmental, and enables you to take personal responsibility.

If you keep these two principles in mind, you should learn many of the specific strategies quite easily.

In this group session, we will review the basic definitions of assertive, passive, and aggressive and make sure that you have a clear understanding of them.

We are presenting assertiveness to you after teaching you about faulty self-talk. *This is because it is much easier to use assertiveness once you realize how your thoughts affect you*. For instance, you might be in the middle of a conflict with your parents, saying to yourself, "They never appreciate anything I do!" As you remember, this is "black and white" thinking. It also means that you're more likely to either feel frustrated and give up (passive) or feel frustrated and become demanding (aggressive).

## COMMUNICATION STYLES

### Passive Style

Giving in to others too easily without making a strong enough effort to see that your *own* wishes, thoughts, and feelings are heard.

### Aggressive Style

Pushing for what you want without regard for other people's feelings. (This may involve putting other people down, accusing, threatening, blaming, yelling, judging, and fighting. )

### Assertive Style

Standing up for yourself and expressing your true feelings, while making an effort to be considerate of other people's feelings, too.

### Conversation in Aggressive Style

Ann: Listen, I've got another bone to pick with you. I've had it with washing and drying dishes. You either pitch in and help me, or I'm going out on strike!

Dan: Lay off now, I'm watching TV.

Ann: Who was your maid last year? You don't care what happens around here, as long as your TV works.

Dan: Don't start that again.

Ann: All you ever do is watch the tube and pump up that tire around your waist.

Dan: Shut up, big mouth!

Notice how Ann starts out by attacking Dan. Ann brings up anger from past situations instead of focusing on asking directly for what she wants now. Nobody wins, because Ann's aggressive style is more focused on hurting Dan and expressing past angers, rather than on requesting his help.

### Conversation in Passive Style

Ann: Pardon me, but would you mind terribly wiping the dishes?
Dan: I'm watching TV.
Ann: Oh, well, all right.

Notice how "Oh, well, all right" rewards Dan for putting Ann off. By reacting passively, Ann fails to get what she wants. She may also view herself as powerless and lose a little bit of her self-respect. She may take it out on Dan indirectly, like burning his meal, being late, or getting angry at something minor.

### Conversation in Assertive Style

Ann: Dan, I'd like some help with the dishes.
Dan: I'm watching TV.
Ann: I would really like us to share the clean-up responsibility. You can get right back to your TV program when we're done.
Dan: They're just about to catch the bad guys.
Ann: Well, I can wait a little while. Will you help me when the program is over?
Dan: Sure, just as soon as it's over.

Notice that Ann was willing to compromise a little, but also stuck with her wish to have Dan help. She didn't stray from the issue by attacking Dan or getting sidetracked by old issues between them.

## ASSERTIVENESS QUIZ

### Scene 1

A: Hey, you're not doing anything, straighten up the room.
B: Do it yourself dummy!

A's behavior is ______ passive ______ aggressive ______ assertive
B 's behavior is ______ passive ______ aggressive ______ assertive

### Scene 2

A: (A is carrying a package that is obviously too large and heavy for one person) Would you mind helping me for a moment?
B: Leave me alone.
A: OK. Sorry.

A's behavior is ______ passive ______ aggressive ______ assertive
B's behavior is ______ passive ______ aggressive ______ assertive

### Scene 3

A (Parent): Why do you always dress like such a slob?
B: I'm sorry that you don't like the way that I dress, but I do.
A: I'm not going to take you anywhere looking like that!!
B: Well, if we're going someplace with your friends, I'll wear those new jeans you got me. When I'm with my friends, I want to dress the way I like.

A's behavior is ______ passive ______ aggressive ______ assertive
B's behavior is ______ passive ______ aggressive ______ assertive

### Scene 4

A: Buy me some fries, will ya?
B: I bought the last couple of times.
A: Thanks a lot, Mr. Scorekeeper.
B: Sorry, but I'm starting to feel taken advantage of.

A's behavior is ______ passive ______ aggressive ______ assertive
B's behavior is ______ passive ______ aggressive ______ assertive

### Scene 5

A: (during a test) Psst, give me the answer to number seven.
B: Shhhh, you'll get us into trouble. I don't think I should.
A: Come on, just show me your paper.
B: OK.

A's behavior is ______ passive ______ aggressive ______ assertive
B's behavior is ______ passive ______ aggressive ______ assertive

### Scene 6

A: I'd really like to go see "Halloween 8."
B: You always pick the movie.
A: If there is something you'd rather see, I'd be willing to consider it.
B: Oh, I don't know. Just go ahead and decide like you always do.

A's behavior is ______ passive ______ aggressive ______ assertive
B's behavior is ______ passive ______ aggressive ______ assertive

**ASSERTIVE BODY LANGUAGE**

1. Maintain direct eye contact.
2. Maintain a good body posture.
3. Speak clearly, audibly, and firmly.
4. Don't whine or use an apologetic tone.
5. Use gestures and facial expression for emphasis.

## FOUR FINGERS

To begin, close your eyes and take several deep and relaxing breaths.

1. Touch your thumb to your index finger. Recall a time when your body felt healthy fatigue, after exhilarating physical activity.

2. Touch your thumb to your middle finger. Recall a very warm and loving experience.

3. Touch your thumb to your ring finger. Recall accepting the nicest compliment you ever received.

4. Touch your thumb to your little finger. Recall the most beautiful place you have ever seen.

GROUP 6

# Active Listening

In order to communicate better with people, you have to be very skilled at listening. Listening does not necessarily mean agreeing. It just means hearing.

Actually, for good communication, you need to do more than just listen. Somehow, you need to communicate to the other person that you really understand what he or she is saying.

One good use for active listening is when you are talking to someone you really care about. Active listening teaches you how to let this person know that you understand. As you know, this is one of the nicest gifts you can offer someone.

Another situation when active listening really helps is when there is some tension between you and someone else. If you let the other person know that you understand how he or she feels, it usually helps.

Today you will learn the basic principles of active listening. Next, you will learn about how *not* to do it. Remember, however, that sometimes, these "errors" are not really errors at all—there is never only one correct way of letting someone know that you are listening. You will also get a chance to role-play and practice these new skills.

## ACTIVE LISTENING

**Purpose:** To let the other person know that you "hear" how he or she "feels."

Think of a time when someone else responded to you in a way that helped you feel free to be yourself and to talk about your feelings. The other person probably communicated some of the following messages:

1. that he or she understood
2. that he or she was genuinely interested in you
3. that he or she wouldn't judge you
4. that he or she had faith in your ability to solve problems

### Mirror

The most basic form of active listening is to *mirror* the other person's feelings with the sentence:

"You sound ____(feeling)____ about ____(situation)____."
or
"You must really feel ____________________."
or
"What you're saying is that ____________________."

### Clarify

Once you have let the other person know that you "hear" what he or she is saying, then it's usually a good idea to ask him or her some questions to *clarify* the situation. You want to encourage the person to say more:

"So, what happened that got you so upset?"
"How did you feel when that happened?"

Remember: The purpose of the questions is to *let the other person know you are concerned and interested*—not just to get information for your own curiosity or gossip.

## ACTIVE LISTENING ERRORS

### Cheering Up

"All I ever do is the dirty work around here. It's not fair!"
"Oh, come on, it's a hot day, you're just in a bad mood, don't worry about it."

### Questioning

"You can't trust anyone around here without getting stabbed in the back!"
"Oh really, who are you talking about? Anyone I know?"

### Oversupporting

"I could die here and no one would notice!"
"Now, now, it's OK. It's all going to be better, I'll help you."

### Defending

"I've been trying to get better at volleyball for three weeks, and now you tell me I have to learn to serve better if I want to play on the team!"
"I'm the captain. I'm in charge. No more discussion!"

### Judging

"I'm supposed to talk to the rest of the group about my drug problem. I've gone over what I want to say but I know they're just going to laugh at me."
"You shouldn't feel that way."

### Parroting

"This place is really disgusting."
"It sounds like you think this place is really disgusting."

## ACTIVE LISTENING ROLE-PLAYING

See if you can come up with some good active listening responses to the following statements. Remember the key principles: *Mirror* and *clarify*.

1. Mother to her children: "Why won't any of you kids ever help me? You don't care about anyone but yourselves!"
2. Teenager to his father: "You can never understand me. You're too old!"
3. Teenager to her counselor: "How come you always get interrupted by phone calls whenever we're supposed to talk?"
4. Staff counselor to a co-worker, after coming out of a meeting with her supervisor: "I work my fingers to the bone around here and I never get anything in return!"
5. Teenager to his older brother: "That school is so stupid. I'm never going back there. Getting an education doesn't matter anyway."

## THE COUNTDOWN

This is a very simple and effective technique. Simply say to yourself, "I am calm and relaxed at the number 10." After your next breath, say "I am even more calm and relaxed at the number 9 than I was at the number 10." After another breath, say, "I am even more calm and relaxed at the number 8 than I was at the number 9" and so on, until you reach the number 1.

GROUP 7

# Asking for Change

From last week's group, you now know the differences among assertive, passive, and aggressive. Today you will be learning some very specific techniques for *asking for change* from other people.

This technique has four steps. You want to be sure to identify a *specific* behavior for the other person to change, rather than changing the whole personality (which is hard to do!). You need to make sure the other person knows exactly how you *feel*. You need to request a specific *change* from the other person—and than let the person know what *positive effect* it will have if he or she can do it.

As with all assertive behavior, the goal here is to communicate, not to accuse.

## ASKING FOR CHANGE

1. Specify the behavior you would like the other person to change.
2. Tell the other person how you feel about this behavior.
3. Name the specific changes you would like to see. Also, what might you need to change in your own behavior?
4. What will you do in response if the other person can make these changes?

1. When you ______________________________
______________________________
______________________________
______________________________

2. I feel ______________________________
______________________________
______________________________
______________________________

3. I wish (I want) ______________________________
______________________________
______________________________
______________________________

4. If you can do that, I will ______________________________
______________________________
______________________________
______________________________

**Examples of *Asking For Change***

| | |
|---|---|
| WHEN YOU . . . | Describe to the other person the exact behavior you find bothersome. Be as objective and specific as possible. |
| POOR | "You're ignoring me! You insensitive, spiteful, obnoxious creep!" |
| BETTER | "When we set up a time to meet somewhere you're often late." |

* * *

| | |
|---|---|
| I FEEL . . . | Express how you feel about the other person's behavior. Make sure you acknowledge that these are *your* feelings. |
| POOR | "You make me so angry I could wring your neck. You are disgusting. I hate you." |
| BETTER | "When you do this my feelings get hurt. I feel that I'm unimportant to you." |

* * *

| | |
|---|---|
| I WISH (I WANT) . . . | Ask clearly for a different, specific behavior. "Please stop doing X and start doing Y." The request must be reasonable and within the power of the other person to meet. |
| POOR | "NOTICE I'M ALIVE!!" |
| BETTER | "I wish you would really make an effort to be on time when we set something up." |

* * *

| | |
|---|---|
| IF YOU CAN DO THAT, I WILL . . . | Spell out the positive effect if the other person can change. This may be as simple as making you feel better. Emphasize the positive consequences whenever possible. |
| POOR | "If you don't, I'll trash your home." |
| BETTER | "I'd feel more respected and our relationship would be better." |

# 3 x 2 x 1*

Partially close your eyes. Finish the sentence, "Right now I am aware of . . . " with the first three things you see. Repeat with three things you hear. Repeat with three physical sensations. Then go through each two times. Then go through each one time.

*Thanks to Dr. Stephen Gilligan for this technique.

GROUP 8

# Special Strategies

(a)

(b)

Now you have a clear picture of assertive communication and you know a number of different strategies to make sure you come across that way.

But, what happens if you go through all the right steps:

(a) you recognize what you are feeling;
(b) you identify the faulty self-talk that makes your feelings more disturbing than they need to be;
(c) you decide what you want to communicate about the problem to someone else;
(d) you review the assertiveness principles and prepare to communicate in a clear, nonaggressive way;
(e) you make sure your assertive body language matches your words;

(c)

(d)

and then the other person still doesn't listen? Or is rude? Or ignores you? Or puts you down? Or changes the subject? Or responds in any other way that doesn't go according to plan?

Before we discuss specific strategies for how to deal with this kind



(e)

of response, it is important to remember one thing: *Expressing yourself with assertive communication is no guarantee of getting your needs met*. It just increases the odds and helps your sense of self-respect.

In today's group you will be learning about special strategies. We all need to know some strategies, in advance, for what to do when people don't respond well to our assertive communication. Also included are ways to deal with other people who are *not* using assertive communication with you.

# SPECIAL STRATEGIES

These techniques will help you avoid becoming sidetracked or manipulated when you make assertive requests.

## Broken Record

Keep your listener from slipping away. Shift back to the issue and calmly repeat your point.

Ann: I'd really like to see "Star Trek" tonight.
Dan: No, let's go to the movie I want to see! Yours is no good.
Ann: Wait a minute. Last time you chose the movie. I'd really like to see my movie this time.
Dan: No, it's stupid. I've got a better one.
Ann: I understand you want to see something else, but I'd really like to see "Star Trek."
Dan: What's the big deal? Who cares whose turn it is? Let's just see my movie!
Ann: I know you want to see yours, but I really want to see this.

## Time-out

Suggest to the other person that you both wait for a less tense time to discuss the problem. Delay responding until people have calmed down and can be more reasonable.

Dan: Mom, it really bothered me when you put me down in front of my friends last night.
Mom: Don't you dare criticize me! I'm going to get you back for this!
Dan: What are you talking about? I'm just trying to tell you something!
Mom: Oh, is that all? Who are you to tell me what to say or do?
Dan: Look, you're too angry at me to talk about this right now. Let's wait till after dinner.
or
Dan: If you threaten me or put me down, we'll never work this out. Let's talk about this later when we're both cooled down.

### State the Importance

Clarify how important this is to you and that you don't want to be brushed aside. This often is effective when used with the Broken Record.

Ann: I'd like to talk to you about what I need to do to get a pass for the weekend.
Dan: Oh yeah, OK, we'll talk about it later. It's no big deal.
Ann: Well, last time we waited too long, and I never got to go. This is really important to me. I'd like to take care of it now.
Dan: I told you not to sweat it. I'll get to it when I can!
Ann: But this is really important to me. Can we set a time to meet so that we make sure to take care of it?

### Admitting Past Errors

Avoid letting the other person sidetrack you with accusations about the past. Admit that you may have made errors in the past, but this is now, and you are trying to handle things better.

Dan: It really bugged me when you got so drunk and aggressive at the party last weekend.
Ann: You're a fine one to talk! You're the one who's always been such a jerk at parties!
Dan: Well, I know I've done that some in the past, but I'm working on it. But right now I want to let you know how I felt about the way you acted.

**Playing Detective**

Ask sincerely about the other person's specific complaints so you can understand and attempt to solve the problem.

Dan: You never care about anybody but yourself!
Ann: You're really mad about something. What did I do that makes you think that?
Dan: You know exactly what I'm talking about!
Ann: I really don't, but I'd like to so that maybe I could do something about it.
Dan: Why the hell didn't you invite me along to that party?
Ann: I had no idea that upset you. Let's talk about this.

## FILLING YOUR ROOM

Let your eyes close and relax. Imagine yourself sitting alone quietly in an empty room. Notice how you feel. Now imagine adding a person or object that you would especially like to have with you in your room. Observe how you feel. Now add someone or something else and observe how you feel. Continue adding people and special objects or decorations to your room until you have filled it to your satisfaction. Pay attention to how full and satisfied you feel.

GROUP 9

# Challenging Your Assertive Skills

Now that you know the five basic special strategies, you need some practice in applying them to different situations. In today's group, we will ask you to identify which of the five special strategies would be the best response to different situations. Then decide on a specific way to say it in this situation. There may be more than one correct answer on some of these—the goal is to get you thinking about new ways to handle these conflicts.

The more you practice, the more possibilities you have available to you when you really need them. The goal here is to increase your options, so you don't have to react the same way all the time.

## TOUGH RESPONSES

Here are some typical responses that will be used to attack or throw off your assertive communication. Which special strategy could you use?

### Laughing It Off

The other person responds with a joke or sarcasm when you make a request.

You: I think I've earned enough points and I've met most of my goals—I'd like to petition to make Level 2.
Response: You want Level 2? I'm not sure how you even made it to Level 1!

Your special strategy:

### The Reversal

The other person responds by attacking you.

You: It really bothers me when you keep interrupting me in these family meetings—please let me finish what I have to say.
Response: Well, what about what you do all the time! Who are you to talk? You're the biggest loudmouth in the family, and you always have been!

Your special strategy:

### Delaying

The person delays when she really could respond to you right away. You get the feeling that she will forget about it.

You: I'd like to sit down and talk about what I need to do to get a pass.
Response: Look, I'm too tired—I don't want to deal with this now. Maybe later.

Your special strategy:

### Self-Pity

The other person tries to make you feel guilty.

You (to your boyfriend): I want to go out with some of my girlfriends Friday night. It's Kathy's birthday, and we really haven't seen each other for a long time.
Response: You don't really love me. You don't care about my needs!

Your special strategy:

### Threats

The other person threatens you with something.

You (to your boyfriend): I want to go out with some of my girlfriends Friday night. It's Kathy's birthday, and we really haven't seen each other for a long time.
Response: If you do that, you're just going to have to find yourself another boyfriend!

Your special strategy:

**Challenging**

The other person tries to put you down for stating your position.

You: I don't want to go to the party with you. I know there will be a lot of drugs there, and I need to stay away from that.
Response: What's wrong with you? You used to be lots of fun! That's stupid!

Your special strategy:

## PROTECTIVE SHELL

With your eyes closed, identify a particular area in your body where you feel safe and confident. Even if you don't feel it now, think back to a time of feeling safe and confident; then remember where in your body the feeling was strongest. Picture a color associated with this physical feeling. Now imagine this feeling radiating out from that spot in your body like a beam of light. Let this beam spread into a "protective shell" around your whole body. Imagine other people trying to hurt you physically or verbally, but you are protected by your "protective shell." Experiment with setting the "protective shell" aside or opening it a crack to let in someone or something that you welcome, then closing it again for self-protection.

GROUP 10

# The Magic Formula*

Think of all the times when you wanted something from an authority figure, like a parent or a teacher or a counselor, and you just couldn't get through.

Often what happens in these situations is that you end up feeling resentful, frustrated, and helpless. The Magic Formula helps you use your self-talk skills and your communications skills so that the other person will hear you better. It doesn't always work, of course—but you can learn some good strategies to help things in the future even when it's not working right now.

You have to figure out what your true goal is here. If your goal is to express all your feelings and to let the world know exactly what you think, then this is probably not the best technique. However, if your goal is to build an alliance with the authority figure and to help get what you need in the long run, then try this.

In today's group, you will practice different situations when the Magic Formula may come in handy.

*Thanks to Dr. John Parker for this model.

## THE MAGIC FORMULA

1. The appreciation
2. The "I" message
3. The detective

**Purpose:** Negotiate so you can get at least SOME of the things you want with an adult, like one of your parents or your teacher.

- The appreciation: "Thanks for caring about me, Mom. I know you must be worried when you tell me I need to be in by 11:00."
- The "I" message: "I would really like to stay out later for this party tonight."
- The detective: "How can I show you I'm ready to handle this? What will it take to get your trust?"

**If you still get "no," your mission is to not disconnect!**

### The Back-up Plans

4. The broken record: "It sounds like you're really not sure I can handle this – how can we work it out?"
5. The future credit: "OK, I can see you don't think I'm ready for this, but I hope you'll take it into consideration the next time. I really want you to trust me again."

## PROGRESSIVE MUSCLE RELAXATION

*Instructions*: Only tense the muscles in one area. Don't overstress the muscle.

A. Take three deep breaths. Relax your stomach.
B. Tense each muscle for a few seconds at a time, then relax for several seconds. Focus on the difference between the muscle when tense and when relaxed.

1. Feet: toes and ankles
2. Calves
3. Thighs
4. Hips
5. Stomach
6. Shoulders
7. Arms: upper, lower, fists
8. Neck
9. Face and scalp

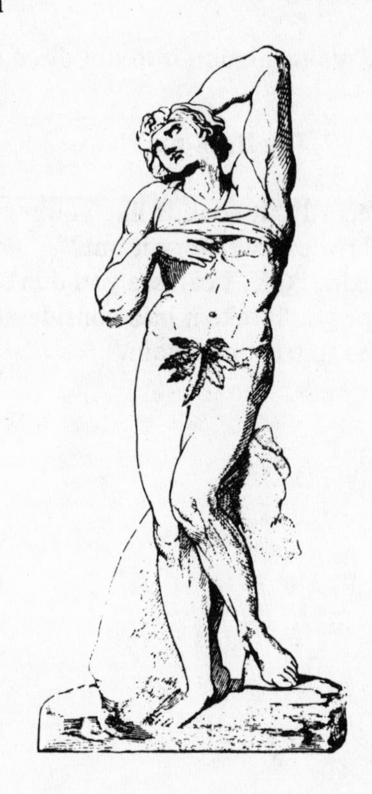

# GROUP 11

# Peer Pressure

Now that you all have more experience dealing with difficult situations, it's time to learn how to apply these skills to some really challenging situations. The situation that we will be working on today is one that is especially tricky for teenagers: peer pressure.

You have all faced situations when other people have tried to talk you into things that you didn't want to do or, even worse, things that part of you really *did* want to do, but you knew would turn out to be harmful or self-destructive.

There are always several options whenever you are faced with one of these situations. You can "go along with the crowd" so that you don't look "chicken" or get anybody mad at you. You can blow up at the people who are trying to talk you into something and lose the friendship.

You can also, following the principles of assertiveness, explain your needs and feelings directly in a way that doesn't put the other person on the defensive.

Like the other skills we teach you, this one is only one option and may not work for you in all situations. Usually, however, people with the highest self-esteem are able to choose this option.

## RESISTING PEER PRESSURE*

Reasons to resist:

1. You stay in control.
2. You stay out of trouble.
3. If you do it respectfully, you may not lose your friends.

Basic rules for your behavior:

1. Resist pressure if you don't feel right about what people are asking you to do.
2. The goal is to express your true needs and feelings in a way that is least likely to cause more conflict or tension. If your "friend" can't respect your point of view even though you say it clearly and without accusations, he or she may not be the right "friend" for you.
3. You may need to try the "Broken Record" technique and/or the "State the Importance" technique if the person doesn't take you seriously at first. However, if he or she persists, the best thing to do is to leave the situation.

Steps:

1. Face the person.
2. Make eye contact.
3. Use a serious voice and facial expression.
4. Remain friendly; see if you can get your point across without putting the other person down.
5. Say no.
6. Give a reason for saying no.
7. Suggest something else to do.
8. Use the "Broken Record" and "State the Importance" technique to get your point across.

*Adapted from J. B. Schumacher et al. (1988). *Social skills for daily living*, Circle Pines, MN: American Guidance Service.

9. If the person does not listen to you, say no again and leave. You don't need to keep defending yourself.
10. Use positive self-talk to reward yourself afterwards.

Role-playing:

1. A friend is upset and tells you she is going AWOL. She insists that you come with her as a sign of support.
2. A friend asks you to let her copy your homework.
3. A friend wants you to skip school all afternoon and go to Tijuana and get stoned.
4. A friend asks you to steal a transistor radio from the store where you work.

## SHELF TECHNIQUE

Sit quietly and imagine yourself sitting alone in a room with a shelf alongside you. Focus on something that is worrying or upsetting you. Pay attention to exactly how your body feels as you think about this. Now imagine this "worry" suddenly leaving your body and floating into the room. Catch the "worry" in your hands and form it into a particular shape, like with a ball of clay, between your hands. Place the object on your shelf, take a deep breath, and say, "Except for this, I am fine." Repeat for as many "worries" as you can identify. When you are finished, imagine yourself looking over at the "worries" on the shelf and say to yourself, "Except for all of these, I am fine."

GROUP 12

# Teasing

In today's group, we will concentrate on another complicated situation that most teenagers have a lot of trouble handling: teasing.

Think of all the different times you have been teased about something. Sometimes teasing, from the right person at the right time, is very affectionate and can actually feel good. At other times, however, teasing can be very aggressive and can feel awful.

The assertive approach to dealing with teasing involves two different skills: knowing what to say to yourself (self-talk) and knowing what to say to the other person. You need to constantly remind yourself that someone with positive self-esteem doesn't put up with aggressive teasing, nor does she give the teaser a lot of power by becoming aggressive or teasing back.

As part of your self-talk, it's also helpful to remember why people tease: usually because of their own insecurity or because they are feeling one-down.

# RESPONDING TO TEASING*

Reasons:

1. Stop the teasing.
2. Gain the respect of others.
3. Gain self-respect.
4. Avoid getting into fights.

Basic rules:

1. Respond to teasing when someone's teasing upsets you. If the teasing is good-natured and doesn't bother you, then you don't need to use these techniques.
2. As with other assertive communications, the goal here is to express your true needs and feelings in a way least likely to cause more conflict and tension.
3. You may need to try the "Broken Record" and/or "State the Importance" if the person doesn't take you seriously at first. However, if he or she persists, the best thing to do is to leave the situation ("Time Out").

Steps:

1. Face the person.
2. Make eye contact.
3. Use a serious voice and facial expression.
4. Ask the person to stop teasing you.
5. Give a reason for the person to stop.
6. Avoid whining; talk confidently.
7. Use "Broken Record" and "State the Importance" to get your point across.
8. If the person stops, say thanks and change the subject. If the person does not stop, leave.
9. Make sure you are using positive self-talk during and after this situation.

*Adapted from J. B. Schumacher et al. (1988). *Social skills for daily living*, Circle Pines, MN: American Guidance Service.

Role-playing:

1. A friend makes fun of the burn marks on your arms that you put there when you were feeling depressed.
2. Your parents tease you about being overweight.
3. A co-worker teases you about being too slow at your work.
4. A teacher makes fun of your last name.
5. Your friends tease you because your girlfriend used to go out with someone else they know.

## BLACKBOARD TECHNIQUE

Sit quietly and take several deep, relaxing breaths. Imagine yourself traveling to a private place where you notice a blackboard. Written on the blackboard are three critical statements that others have made about you in the past. Notice how you feel when you read these. Walk up to the blackboard, erase the statements, and write three positive statements about yourself in response. Notice how you feel when you read them. Take a deep breath and remind yourself that you can make these positive statements to yourself whenever you need to.

GROUP 13

# Compliments

Today's group deals with compliments. There is an assertive way to respond to compliments that is direct and rewarding. This is different from the nonassertive and insecure ways of responding to compliments.

Every compliment that is offered to you is an opportunity to feel good about yourself. It is also an opportunity to make the other person feel rewarded for offering you something positive. The assertive response to compliments is called "Accept and Reward." With the right response, you feel good inside, and the odds that the other person will compliment you again increase.

The problem for most people in accepting compliments has to do with faulty self-talk. If you feel bad about yourself, compliments are hard to accept because they don't match your view of yourself. If you've been trained to believe that you will be put down if you ever feel proud, you will automatically deflect compliments. If you have been betrayed and manipulated by others, you may be suspicious of their compliments.

In this exercise, we will divide into groups of two. Each person will give three compliments to his or her partner and simply observe how the partner reacts. Does he deflect it? Does she seem suspicious? Does she immediately return the compliment? Does he ignore it? Or does he accept it? An important observation to make is within yourself: Do you feel like giving another compliment to your partner based on his or her response? Remember—this exercise is not concerned with how to give compliments, but rather with how to receive them.

## DEALING WITH COMPLIMENTS

Accepting compliments well is one sign of assertiveness, which can help us manage our stress. The purpose of this exercise is to examine what happens to us when we are given a sincere compliment and when we give one to another person.

### Response Possibilities

1. *Accept and Reward*: This is the most assertive and nonstressful response to compliments. This usually means saying "Thanks . . . I appreciate that" and looking pleased. The key to this style is that you feel good and you make the *other* person feel good for complimenting you.

The following responses are "defensive" responses and may cause us to miss the opportunity for feeling good.

2. *Accept and Give Back the Compliment*: This is a common way we deal with the embarrassment we may feel when we are complimented. "Oh, thanks, you look nice too!"
3. *Deflect*: Watch for nonverbal signs of deflection such as tossing the compliment away with the eyes or a shrug of the shoulders.
4. *Refuse*: "Oh, this old thing?" or "Well, I really am not doing that well," etc. This kind of refusal gives the other person the message that they are wrong or that their perceptions are off. They are not likely to continue complimenting us.
5. *Become Suspicious of Others' Motives*: Often we learn that other people will try to manipulate us with compliments. If this has been done to you in the past you may be suspicious even when there is no reason to be. You may wonder "Why is she trying to flatter me? What does he want?"

   Sometimes it makes sense to be suspicious, but many times it is just one more way of losing out on an opportunity to feel good.
6. *Big Shot*: Because the compliment makes you nervous, you cover it up and say "I know I'm the strongest dude in town." Nobody wants to give more compliments to someone who acts this way.

## VIBRATING SYMBOL*

Focus on the area in your body where you notice discomfort when you feel upset, hurt, or anxious. Now imagine a symbol or image that almost always has a soothing, calming effect on you (a special person, a special place, an object that has special meaning to you, etc.). Close your eyes and sit quietly. Picture your special symbol somewhere in the room and imagine that it is very slightly vibrating and alive. With each breath, imagine it moving steadily closer to you, drawn directly to the spot you have chosen where you feel discomfort or tension. When the symbol reaches the surface of your body, imagine it passing right through your skin and into the tense area that needs soothing. Feel the soothing, strengthening quality of this vibrating symbol. Take a few moments to enjoy the effects.

*Thanks to Dr. Stephen Gilligan for this technique.

GROUP 14

# The Four-Square*

This group session concentrates on how to make decisions.

Try thinking of all decisions that you make in several different ways. First think about the long-term effects and the short-term effects. Next think about the effect on yourself and the effect on other people who matter to you.

With the Four-Square, you have a map that can guide you in making smart decisions. If the effect of a decision is probably going to be positive now *and* in the future, it is probably a good move. If it will be positive both for you and others, it is a super good move.

Plenty of times, however, a decision is only good for you right now; it may be bad for you later, and bad for other people. It might be time to think twice about your choice.

Many teenagers insist that they aren't able to stop and think before doing things—they just happen. It often seems that way, but most of you are capable of "slowing time down" and making intelligent choices.

*Thanks to Dr. John Parker for this model.

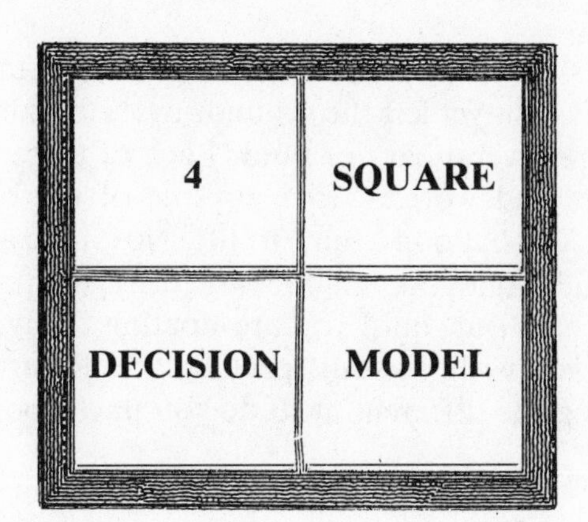


When you use this, you make four separate decisions about some choice. Each one answers this question: "Is it a good decision for you in this time frame?"

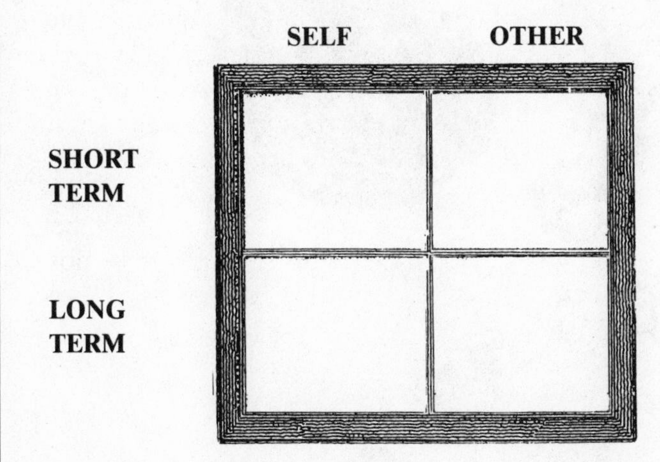

## THE SANDBAG TECHNIQUE

Close your eyes and sit quietly. Visualize yourself standing in a hot-air balloon that has not yet left the ground. In the basket of the balloon along with you are several bags of sand. Each of these bags represents different anxieties and worries. Pick up one of the bags and toss it onto the ground. The balloon begins to lift. Now take another bag and toss it out. The balloon becomes lighter and drifts off further. Continue tossing different bags out, until you are floating freely, free of worry. You can land, if you wish, in your special place. Return whenever you are ready, noticing the different attitude you have about your worries when you return.

## GROUP 15

# Cue Therapy

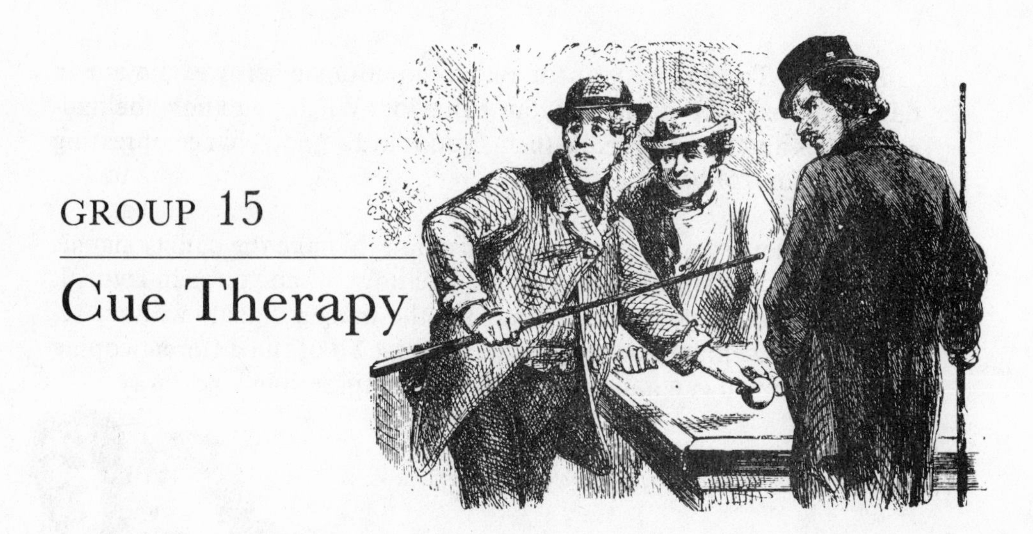

You have all learned many different strategies for coping with difficult situations. By the time you leave these sessions, you will know how to look at things differently, and you will have many tools for handling things differently.

You're still going to face tough situations that will serve as cues for you to go back to an old behavior pattern. This might mean going to a party where you are offered drugs or maybe someone at school will tease you about your looks. Because of previous conditioning, we are each wired to respond in old ways to these cues.

Cue Therapy prepares you to do some new things in these familiar situations. Actors in a play or movie train themselves to react just the way they want to right after their cue. So do athletes, when they try to anticipate a game situation.

In Cue Therapy, you will rehearse very specific ways to deal with the toughest cues. If you think about it, you'll find that you know what these tough cues are. Here is your chance to use your self-talk, your imagery, your communication skills, your problem solving, and anything else that works for you to help you meet your goals. The more dramatic and real you can make it in the group, the more prepared you will be when you face the real situation.

## CUE THERAPY

**Purpose:** To prepare you for future situations when you may be in danger of losing control over your behavior. When you know the danger signals and how to handle them, you stand a good chance of getting your self-control back.

**Technique:** Use role-play or visualization to make the danger signals (known as "cues" in PRISM) real for you now, when you're in control. The key is to let yourself feel and see the danger signals without responding to them in old ways. Next, rehearse all of the different coping strategies so you can handle the dangerous situation in a new way.

### Coping Strategies

1. Scare yourself/Support yourself
   (a) Example: Think back to how TERRIBLE your body felt after using crystal the last time you did it. Really let all the gory details come to mind, and focus on how BAD it felt.
   (b) Then focus right away on a really positive image, something that will immediately make you feel better, or imagine a special place you can escape to. Think of the positive result if you can deal with this impulse.
2. Visualization/Relaxation
3. Fun: Plan to do something that feels good whenever you get those urges.
4. Self-talk: Talk to yourself, and call upon your ally and Supportive Observer to help.
5. Talk to a friend: Call a friend, therapist, sponsor or family member who can help you.

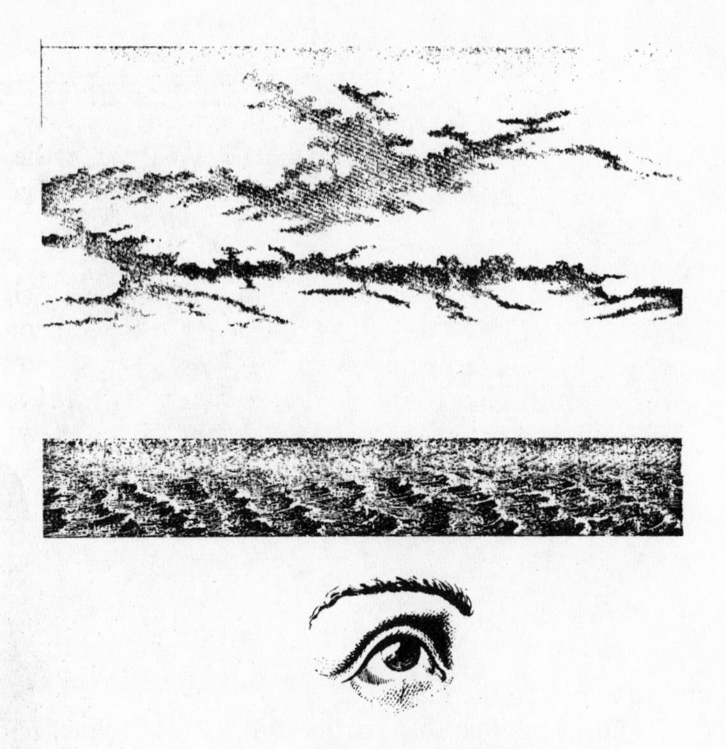

**THE HORIZON SYMBOL**

Think of someone or something that has a very soothing and calming effect on you. Visualize this image as being very far away, just barely visible on the horizon. As you count backwards from 10 to 1, picture your image gradually moving closer to you. The closer it gets, the more clearly you can see it. At the same time, you notice the calming effect as its presence is nearer to you. At the count of 1, this person or thing is so close you can reach out and touch it. Notice the effect of having this image so close and supportive to you.

GROUP 16

# Back to the Future

Now it's time to look into the future.

All of you who have gone through the full PRISM sequence have learned many different approaches to problem-solving. You have learned how to control your body's responses to stress. You have learned how to use your ally and Supportive Observer to talk to yourself in helpful ways. You have learned how to ask for what you need from others directly without being aggressive. You have learned strategies for how to hang in there when others are making it difficult for you. You have learned how to handle peer pressure and teasing. And you have learned how to accept compliments.

Today is your day to enter the Time Machine and discover how you will be able to use these new abilities in the future. With this technique, one of you will choose a date in the future (usually a year from today or your next birthday). We will all help transport you forward in time to that date. When you arrive, we will interview you about how your life is on this future date. First we will find out how you are handling things; then we will ask you how you got there.

## POSITIVE END-RESULT IMAGERY

Before you start, choose a situation you are likely to encounter in the very near future that you would like to handle more successfully then you have in the past. This could be an athletic performance, public speaking, resisting an offer to use drugs, handling yourself in a family therapy session, etc. Now close your eyes and slowly count backwards, from ten to one on every exhale. Now imagine the situation in the future as vividly as possible, including sights, sounds, taste, smells, feelings, thoughts, etc. Observe yourself, as in a slow-motion movie, performing the task successfully. Study carefully what steps you are taking to help yourself be more successful. Remember to make the accomplishment realistic—you may even imagine minor failures in addition to overall success. The more clearly you can imagine the successful performance, the more probable it will be that you can do the same thing in reality. This requires repetition and practice.

## RELAXATION AND VISUALIZATION TECHNIQUES

The following is a list of successful relaxation and visualization techniques, in addition to the ones already included in the group sessions. Experiment with each of them to see which work the best for you. They are described here to remind you of some of the different possibilities open to you.

### Autogenics

Close your eyes. Repeat the following sentences to yourself:

1. "My right arm is warm and heavy."
2. "My left arm is warm and heavy."
3. "Both of my arms are warm and heavy."

This series should be repeated *very* slowly, three times, until you actually experience some of the warmth and heaviness. Mental imagery may be combined with this technique.

### Arm Levitation

Close your eyes and rest your hands on your knees. Imagine lightness in one of your hands, as if being pulled up into the air by balloons attached to your wrists. Let your hand slowly lift and float, as if pulled by the balloons, or imagine a powerful magnet pulling your hand higher. Let your hand drift higher and higher towards your face. When your hand touches a particular spot on your face, you know that you are deeply relaxed.

## Quieting Reflex

1. Become aware of worry or stress—this is the cue to start.
2. Smile inwardly with your mouth and eyes, and say to yourself, "alert mind, calm body." Repeat several times.
3. Inhale an easy, natural breath, while mentally counting "1, 2, 3"; then exhale, counting "1, 2, 3."
4. While exhaling, let your jaw, tongue, and shoulders go loose. Feel aware of heaviness and warmth flowing to your toes as you let your breath out.

## Bubble Technique

Close your eyes and sit quietly. Imagine yourself floating underwater with a full air supply, with no tensions, and with no need to support yourself. Whenever you notice a thought, picture it as an air bubble in the water and watch as it just floats away and disappears. Continue with each thought until the water and your thoughts become very peaceful. This same technique can be used with the imagery of sitting on a riverbank and watching logs roll by, or sitting in front of a campfire and watching puffs of smoke disappear into the air.

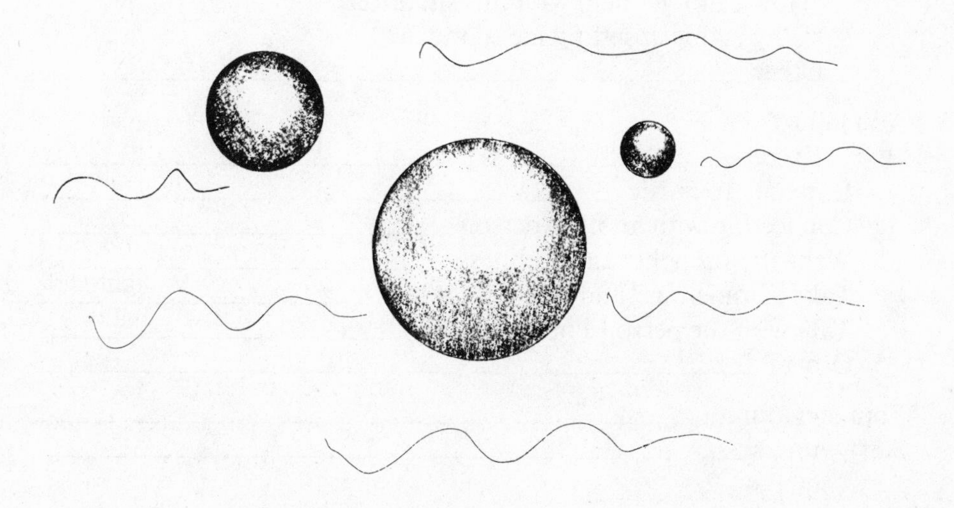

## COPING WITH STRESS WORKSHEET

We want you to become very familiar with your personal coping style during frustrating or stressful times. It's really important to understand your "trigger," the event that sent your over the edge into some action you later felt bad about.

WHAT WAS YOUR TRIGGER EVENT? ____________________
______________________________________________
______________________________________________

### SO HOW DID YOU COPE?
### (WHAT NEW OPTIONS DID YOU USE?)

RELAXATION TECHNIQUE

stairway____ $3 \times 2 \times 1$____ falling leaf____
10-candle____ 5-finger____ relaxation tape____
deep breathing____ progressive muscle____
visual imagery (describe) ____________________
______________________________________________

SELF-TALK

"What do I need to do to take care of myself?"
"How did I cope with this before?"
"How can I get help with this situation?"
"Why is this upsetting me so much?"
Other ____________________

ACTIVITY

Exercise ____________________
Listening to music ____________________
Connecting with another person ____________________
Write my thoughts and feelings ____________________
Take a "time-out" and deal with it later ____________________
Talk with the person I'm upset with ____________________
Other ____________________

Your signature ____________________
Staff witness ____________________

## CUE THERAPY WORKSHEET

Cue: ____________________________________________

### My Coping Strategies

1. Scare myself this way: ______________________________

______________________________________________

______________________________________________

   Support myself this way: ______________________________

______________________________________________

______________________________________________

2. My favorite relaxation technique (body control): ______________

______________________________________________

______________________________________________

3. Fun things that will really help to distract me: ______________

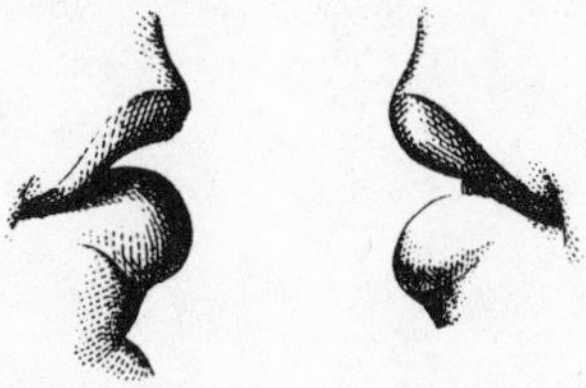

______________________________________________

______________________________________________

4. The self-talk that really works for me: ______________________

______________________________________________

______________________________________________

5. Who to call when I need to reach out: ______________________

______________________________________________

______________________________________________